Money Management 101

How to Save More, Get Out of Debt and Create Financial Security

© Copyright 2020 - All rights reserved.

The content contained within this book may not be reproduced, duplicated or transmitted without direct written permission from the author or the publisher.

Under no circumstances will any blame or legal responsibility be held against the publisher, or author, for any damages, reparation, or monetary loss due to the information contained within this book, either directly or indirectly.

Legal Notice:

This book is copyright protected. It is only for personal use. You cannot amend, distribute, sell, use, quote or paraphrase any part, or the content within this book, without the consent of the author or publisher.

Disclaimer Notice:

Please note the information contained within this document is for educational and entertainment purposes only. All effort has been executed to present accurate, up to date, reliable, complete information. No warranties of any kind are declared or implied. Readers acknowledge that the author is not engaging in the rendering of legal, financial, medical or professional advice. The content within this book has been derived from various sources. Please consult a licensed professional before attempting any techniques outlined in this book.

By reading this document, the reader agrees that under no circumstances is the author responsible for any losses, direct or indirect, that are incurred as a result of the use of information contained within this document, including, but not limited to, errors, omissions, or inaccuracies.

CONTENTS

Introduction	1
Part One- How to Save More	
Chapter 1: Goal Setting	5
Chapter 2: Budgeting	11
Chapter 3: Spend Less and Make More	17
Part Two – Get Out of Debt	
Chapter 4: Understand Your Credit Score	23
Chapter 5: All About Credit Cards	29
Chapter 6: Secured and Unsecured Debts	35
Part Three – Create Financial Security	
Chapter 7: The Best Way to Borrow Money	41
Chapter 8: Making Wise Investments	47
Chapter 9: Preparing for Retirement	55
Conclusion	61
References	65

Introduction

When you were growing up, you probably thought of money as a means to an end. If you wanted to buy a car, you would pick up an extra shift and save up to make it happen. But later on in life, as your responsibilities became more complicated, you probably began to see money in a different light. As money becomes more important, you also need to realize the importance of financial security. In today's highly demanding world, It's hard to feel good and live peacefully when you know that you can't provide a comfortable life for your family. The truth is that many people don't fully understand that it's not about having a hefty paycheck at the end of the month, it's a matter of efficient financial management, and that is exactly what this book can help you achieve.

The book is divided into three sections, embodying the pillars of financial management. The first section is dedicated to saving money. In chapter 1, you will learn about the importance of goal setting, along with tips on how you can do that yourself. Chapter 2 is all about budgeting, and you'll read about simple budgeting models and how to use different tools like budgeting apps to create a budget that fits your specific needs. Chapter 3 is where we will discuss how you can spend less and earn more, bringing the first section full circle. In the second section of this book, chapters 4 through 6, it'll all be about getting rid of your debt to start your financial journey anew. You'll learn about credit score, how it affects your financial options, and how to best use your credit cards in a more efficient manner. You will also learn the difference between secure and unsecured debts in chapter 6. The third and final section of this book will guide you towards achieving financial security. You will not only discover how to borrow money, but you'll also benefit from professional advice on making wiser investments and preparing for your retirement. Finally, all the ideas and insights shared in this book will be summarized in the conclusion, and you will be able to review the key points discussed throughout the book.

Think of this book as a trustworthy financial

advisor that you can go back to during different phases of your finance management journey. The best way to work through the different topics discussed here is with a pen and paper and an open mind. Take notes and compare your current financial status against the optimum situations described in every chapter. This way, you'll be able to apply what you're learning as you go for the best results. You will find that you'll want to reach for this book time after time when things start to get out of control, and you need some help to organize your thoughts. Even if you believe that your finances are in tip-top shape, you'll still find something valuable in this book. After all, it's never too late to start thinking about new ways to enhance your financial situation.

Part One- How to Save More

Chapter 1: Goal Setting

Setting achievable goals can increase your chances of success. This is especially true when it comes to achieving financial stability. Research shows that 56% of American households that have a solid financial plan were able to successfully meet their savings goals, compared to 24% of households with no plan. Whether you want to put money aside for a rainy day or save up to buy that dream house, you need to have a strategy in place to achieve your goals. But before you decide how to get there, you must first think about what you want, when you want it, and why. It's perfectly natural to feel overwhelmed when you're trying to prioritize your financial goals. This chapter will walk you through the necessary steps to set specific targets and manage your finances wisely.

Find Your Inspiration

How do you define security and success? The answer to this question will dictate the path you need to take to get there and the milestones you need to cross off your list on the way. For many, security is having a retirement fund or enough savings that they never have to worry about money when they are no longer working. For others, success is leading a luxurious lifestyle, complete with a big house, fancy car, and all that jazz. Think about where you want to be and set goals that align with your aspirations. Visualize your goals and attach reasons to them to help fuel your motivation. Make sure you leave room for immediate, short-term goals in your money management plan. For example, if your ultimate goal is to have a fairytale wedding, then you'll want to set up a savings account so that you can easily save up the necessary funds to cover the cost.

Assess Your Current Situation

Once you have a rough idea of what you want, you need to examine your current situation. Even if you don't have specific goals just yet, taking a long and hard look at where you stand financially can help point you in the right direction. Start by assessing your income, outstanding debts, back taxes, monthly expenses, and net worth. These five financial points are the cornerstones on which your money management plan will be based. Your credit score can help give you a quick overview of your financial health, so make sure you check it and prioritize your goals accordingly. A high score gives you more flexibility when setting financial goals, while a low score will force you to focus on specific targets before you can achieve your lifelong dreams.

Set Short-Term Goals

Setting short-term goals can help give you the confidence and financial boost you need to achieve bigger goals down the line. These first steps are fundamental for your long-term financial stability. You can't make a few thousand dollars appear in your savings account overnight, but you can create a budget that will keep your spending in check, and that will help create a decent emergency fund in only a year; a small change can make a big difference. With a budget in place, you can avoid overspending and build a financial safety net that you can fall back on should you ever find yourself in an unexpected financial rut. Besides establishing a budget and an emergency fund, paying off your credit card debt is another important goal that should be part of your short-term plan. This is because the interest can build exponentially, making it extremely difficult to achieve any other financial goals.

Keep Your Dreams in Mind

Once you've made progress in your short-term plan, you can start working toward achieving your mid-term goals. These can include things like buying your first home, going on the trip of a lifetime, renovating your house, starting a college fund for your children, saving up for your dream wedding, etc. After figuring out your goals, start calculating how much money you need to reach them. When you make a good dent in your short-term goals, achieving your lifelong dreams will become that much easier.

Set Long-Term Financial Goals

The ultimate long-term goal for most people is saving enough money so that they don't have to worry about finances when retirement comes along. Even if you're decades away from retiring, you need to start saving as early as possible, so you have enough money to live comfortably when the time comes. Most financial experts recommend that you save 10% to 15% of every paycheck and put it into a retirement fund. This is the basic rule of thumb, but your retirement fund will depend on your particular needs at the end of the day. If your employer offers a 401(k) and matches your contributions, make sure you take full advantage of that.

Make Sure Your Goals Are SMART

After figuring out your goals, you need to think about the steps you have to take to achieve them. For any financial plan to succeed, you have to make sure your goals are SMART: specific, measurable, achievable, realistic, and time-bound. For example, if you want to save up for a vacation, start by figuring out the details before moving forward. This includes choosing a destination, deciding on when to go, and estimating the trip's total cost. Make the details as specific as possible. That way, you can decide whether this is a practical move, given your current income, savings, and regular expenses. If the goal seems out of reach, try to make adjustments before dismissing the idea completely. You might still be able to go on your dream vacation if you push the deadline back a little, open a new saving account with a higher interest rate, make your trip shorter, or choose a cheaper destination. Keep the plan realistic, and use that to measure the success. In this example, the measuring part is simple. Did you have enough to go on the trip? If you did, it is successful. And be sure to set a time frame. If it will take you a year to save, plan for that, and aim to do it sooner.

Setting short-term, mid-term, and long-term goals are the first step toward securing your financial future. If you aren't working to achieve specific targets, then there's nothing to stop you from spending more than you should. In return, you might find yourself short on money when you need it most, whether it's for unexpected bills, retirement, a medical emergency, etc. Or worse, you might get stuck in a vicious cycle of debt that keeps you from living comfortably. The above steps will point you in the right direction and help you to set immediate and future goals that will help you save more money, live more comfortably within your means, and, ultimately, achieve financial stability.

Chapter 2: Budgeting

To be able to manage your finances, increase your savings, and achieve your immediate and future financial goals, you need a balanced budget. A personal or household budget is a financial plan that tracks your spending and compares your regular income and expenses for a specific period. While this is a crucial step for proper money management and long-term financial stability, many people are reluctant to create a budget, let alone stick to one, because they associate it with restricted spending. However, a budget doesn't necessarily have to be constrictive to be effective; it is not about limiting the fun in your life. A sound budget should be flexible enough to allow you to treat yourself from time to time while helping you control your spending and make the most of every dollar. Here's how budgeting works.

Choose a Budgeting Tool

First off, you need to either find or create a template that you can use to fill in the numbers for your monthly income and expenses. You can use the old-fashioned pen and paper approach, but it's a lot easier to use a budgeting app or a monthly budget spreadsheet. These will include designated sections for income and expenses in various categories, as well as built-in algorithms that help you calculate any surplus or shortfall in your budget with minimal effort, making the process more efficient, accurate, and convenient.

Get Your Financial Paperwork in Order

Next, you need to gather up all your financial paperwork, including your recent bank statements, utility bills, investment accounts, paychecks, mortgage or loan statements, credit card bills, wage and tax statements, 1099 forms, as well as receipts from the past three months. Basically, you'll want to gather any information you can get about your income and expenses and then calculate a monthly estimate for your budget. The more information you can dig up, the better.

Calculate Your Income

How much is your average income per month? If you work a steady job where you receive regular paychecks with automatic tax deductions, you can use the budget's net income amount. On the other hand, if you are self-employed, receive variable income from side gigs, or have additional income sources besides your job, such as Social Security or child support, you'll need to include these in your budget as well. Consider using the total income from your lowest-earning month as a baseline when setting up your financial plan for a reliable budget.

List Your Monthly Expenses

Since a budget is all about controlling your spending, you need to create a list of all your expected monthly expenses. These include car payments, rent or mortgage payments, insurance, student loans, savings, utilities, groceries, childcare, entertainment, eating out, travel expenses, transportation costs, and personal care. You can use your receipts or credit card statements from the last two or three months to track your spending.

Categorize Your Expenses

Now that you have all the expenses you can expect each month; you need to divide them into two categories: fixed and variable. Fixed expenses are those where you pay the same amount each time, such as mortgage or rent payments, regular childcare, standard credit card payments, and set-fee services like your internet package. If you plan to set aside a specific amount of money for a rainy day or pay off a certain amount of debt every month, then you should include those in your fixed-expenses list as well. Your variable expenses, on the other hand, are those that will change from one month to another, such as utilities, groceries, gifts, entertainment, etc.

If you don't have an emergency fund, then you'll want to include a third category for unexpected expenses that might pop up and throw your monthly budget off balance. Next, assign a spending limit to each category, starting with your fixed expenses. For an accurate and realistic estimate, check your credit card or bank transactions from the last couple of months to get a rough estimate of the amount you spend in each category.

Compare Your Income and Expenses

If your average income is more than your expenses, then you're off to a great start. This means that you can allocate the extra money to areas in your budget, such as a retirement fund, a savings account, or loan payments. To manage your finances wisely when you make more than you spend, consider following the "50-30-20" budgeting plan. In a 50-30-20 budget, you spend roughly 50% of your after-tax income on your needs, 30% on your wants, and 20% on debt repayment and savings. On the other hand, if your monthly expenses exceed your average income, that means you're overspending and need to make adjustments to your lifestyle, spending habits, or both, which brings us to the next point.

Track Your Budget and Expenses

If you find that your expenses are higher than your income, you'll need to examine your budget and find areas in the variable expenses category where you can make cut backs. Look for ways to control your spending by cooking your own food instead of eating out, for example. You might also have to consider eliminating non-essential expenses; for instance, you can cancel your gym membership. If your expenses exceed your income tremendously, you have no choice but to reduce your fixed expenses or find a way to increase your income to balance your budget. All in all, you should aim for the income and expenses columns to at least be equal. This means that all your income is accounted for and used to achieve a financial goal.

Now that you know how to create a budget, it's important to keep in mind that it will only work if you're honest about your spending habits. When you have detailed and accurate information about your income and expenses, you will be able to create an effective budget that shows you where your money is coming from, how much you have, how much you owe, and where it all goes each month. Make sure to monitor your expenses in each category every month so you can avoid overspending, identify any problematic spending habits, and cut any unnecessary expenses. That way, you will be able to control your spending and stay on track with your financial goals.

Chapter 3: Spend Less and Make More

Being a responsible spender is a habit that one can develop over time. The majority of people are told from a young age that they need to save money if they want to afford to buy the things they need. Those who applied that piece of advice as they grew older are the ones who are able to manage their finances a little better than others. Earning money is a privilege that many of us have, and it is only right that we get to spend some of that money, especially on luxuries, but there is a fine line between treating yourself and spending cash irresponsibly just because you can. If you want more money, you need to either earn more or spend less. Here is how you can manage your finances better and save your money by spending less.

Review Your Expenditures

Many people do not even realize how much they spend throughout the month or year until they see their bank balance. It is easy to spend a bit here and there, especially when you are using credit or debit, but that spending is not seen until later, and it soon adds up. That often leaves people surprised at how little is left in their account at the end of the month. To avoid being in that situation and to try to manage your finances better, it is crucial that you take time to review your expenditure and see what you can cut loose or avoid altogether. You could be spending too much money on luxurious items when you could find cheaper replacements or are getting charged for something you do not necessarily use anymore. By reviewing every penny that goes in and out of your bank account or wallet, you will be able to make wiser choices when it comes to saving your money and spend less on the things that are only putting you into debt.

Find Discounts

Changing your financial habits for the better requires effort. People tend to spend a lot of extra money on items and services that they can easily get for less if they simply did more research and looked for discounts. There are many goods and services out there, and that means that there is often a cheaper competitor where you can buy the same thing for less. By finding the best deals and opting for discounted items and services, not only will you be spending less of your valuable money, but by the end of the month or year, that money will be available to cut down on your debt or to buy something that you really need in your life.

Use Cash

Psychology plays a huge part in how much a person spends in one place or on a single shopping trip. People do not always realize that when they spend money using their debit or prepaid cards, and they often spend a lot more money than they would if they were using cash. Retailers and service providers are well aware of that fact and do not shy away from using it for their gains. That is why if you are looking to spend less money the next time you go out, or if you are trying to limit your expenditure on online purchases, you need to opt for cash rather than card spending. By forcing yourself to use physical cash, you see a tangible asset that is escaping your grasp, helping you to spend less.

Be Flexible with Choices

Brands are very smart when it comes to advertising their products and making customers think their products are better than those of the competition.

Sometimes, the quality of the products or services really does differ from one brand to another. In most cases, it can come down to who can better market their brand, regardless of quality. Those wanting to spend less and save more should be fully aware of those tricks and use online reviews to source the products that actually work. If the quality is the same or good enough to give you what you need, then consider choosing the cheaper brands rather than the expensive, better-known ones.

Reduce Credit Card Usage

Debt tends to attract even more debt if an end is not put to this vicious cycle. An important step that you should take if you are trying to spend less money and start saving more is to reduce your credit card debt. If you have more than one credit card, then consider cutting down to just one or two so that you can keep up with their loans. You can often transfer balances from one credit card to another to consolidate credit card debt and take advantage of cheaper rates. Having a credit card is essential to improve your credit score, but you will have to make sure you are keeping up with the regular payments to not end up paying more money on huge interest rates that you are better off without.

Browse for Used Items

Nowadays, choosing used items and reusing them is becoming more and more popular, especially with people who are more conscious about their personal impact on the planet. Browsing for used items is not just great for saving the environment; it is also beneficial when it comes to saving your cash. There are tons of products and items out there that are in perfect or near-perfect condition and are being sold much cheaper than new goods. These products offer the same functionality, help the environment, and help to balance your budget.

Being financially aware and thinking twice before spending your money on just anything is the first step towards saving more money. It might take a bit of effort to change your spending habits, but after a while, it will become second nature to you, and you will learn how to be more responsible. It all comes down to making wiser choices without having to cut the luxury items out of your budget.

Part Two – Get Out of Debt

Chapter 4: Understand Your Credit Score

Managing your money starts by becoming financially aware. One of the steps that anyone should take to gain better financial awareness is to understand how the credit score system works and how that affects them. Several elements make up a credit score, and many factors affect each individual. It can be challenging at first for some people to understand how credit scores work or how to calculate it. However, by doing research and spending money more responsibly, one can easily understand and manage their credit score for healthier financial stability. Here is everything you need to know about credit scores and how to manage them.

What is a Credit Score?

Dealing with banks is something that everyone has to do, be it by creating accounts, borrowing money, or anything else related to your finances. Since different banks offer a variety of services to their clientele, they need to establish eligibility criteria to minimize the risks of lending money. The credit score system is exactly what helps banks rank people to how financially responsible and stable they appear to be based on their banking history.

Credit Report Information

Identifying someone's credit score comes from taking a look at their credit report information. Basically, a credit report holds all the banking history a person has and what pattern they appear to show when it comes to dealing with their finances over the years. The report has personal information about the person like their name, address, and employment details. You can also find any recent financial activity on the report, including any open loans, credit inquiries, and anything else that can be found on the person's public record. All of this information can then be used by the bank to determine whether the person is eligible for loans or other services provided by the financial entity.

Types of Credit Scores

If you are looking to borrow money from any lender, you must first understand how they will make their decision. Each entity's criteria to determine whether the person applying for a loan will be successful differs from one place to another. Here are the two main types of credit scores that lenders often use to make their decisions:

Generic

This is the most popular type of credit score and is used by the majority of lenders and businesses. The generic score assesses risk and makes it easy for lenders to make a decision about anyone who is applying for credit and is based on readily available information. In fact, you can also access much of this information, and it is beneficial to take a look before applying to your bank.

Custom

Private individual lenders often use this type of credit score. The custom credit score takes into consideration extra information other than that provided on a regular credit. While regular credit scores are generic to each lender, a custom score will only take into account the information relevant to the credit being applied for. This means that it is more difficult to generate your own custom score as you may not know what is included in the criteria.

Factors Affecting Credit Scores

Credit scores can change over time, depending on a person's spending habits. To maintain a healthy credit score and aim for financial stability, you must understand all the factors affecting your score. Below are some of the factors and how to deal with them to elevate your score over time:

Debt

One of the main factors affecting anyone's credit score is the amount of debt they have. Whether you have a large amount of debt or only have a little, your debt still largely affects your credit score and is written into your credit report. Being in debt to any entity makes any person a risk for lenders, which often causes them to decline their applications. In order to improve your chances of successfully borrowing money and having better financial stability, you need to settle any outstanding debts, and your score will slowly start improving.

Credit Report Inquiries

Whenever a person inquires about their personal credit score, it goes on their credit report and negatively affects it. This is what is known as a hard credit inquiry, and can be visible to any entity where you apply to borrow money. However, certain types of soft inquiries do not necessarily go on one's report or have a negative effect. Those are often requested by individuals merely to check on their financial status without actually applying to get any credit from an entity. In essence, any time you apply for something that requires a credit check, it can affect your credit score. So limit your applications to make sure that you are not set up for failure when you apply.

Payment History

A person's payment history affects their credit score and financial stability. If an individual is up to date with all their payments and never late for any of them, they will usually have a higher credit score than that of a person who misses a few payments here and there. Lenders look at this and ask, "Why would they pay me on time if they are not paying other people on time?". To counteract this, you should pay at least the minimum amount on your debts each month to include this prompt payment in your credit score.

Your credit score may not seem like a big deal if you do not understand how it works and how it affects your life, but once you do, you will see how it can play a huge role in your financial stability. A person's credit report will be pulled every so often when an application for credit from a lender is made, payment plans are set up, and other instances where cash advances are made available. If the score on that report does not turn out to be high enough, the borrowing request may be denied, and it can be really frustrating for the borrower. In order to avoid this issue, make sure you research and keep up with your credit score by making more responsible financial choices.

Chapter 5: All About Credit Cards

By now, you should understand that credit cards aren't the answer to your financial struggles. Whether you've experienced it yourself or seen someone else go through it, drowning yourself in credit card debt can push you into bankruptcy. However, when used mindfully, having access to credit cards can sometimes be the lifeline you need. This chapter will teach you about different types of credit cards and when to use each of them. You will also find out how to form a healthier relationship with your credit cards and use them efficiently to get out of debt. Let's start with the basics:

How Do Credit Cards Work?

Credit cards were first introduced back in the mid-90s when major department stores adopted the then-new system to increase their customers' loyalty rather than their convenience. By allowing them to buy now and pay later, their customers started buying more than ever. Other businesses started to take notice of how successful this model was, and the rest is history. It was a winning deal for everyone. Consumers had access to funds they didn't physically own, business owners made profits, and banks, playing the role of a middleman, were granted a golden opportunity to get a piece of the action. Although, as it turned out, it was an enormous chunk rather than just a piece!

Types of Credit Cards

With time, different types of credit cards were created to serve consumers' more elaborate financial needs. Below you will find information about the various types of credit cards and how you can use each to fulfill your specific needs.

1. Standard Credit Cards

Standard credit cards are the most typical and common types of credit cards. Providing a basic no interest benefit as long as you settle your monthly balance before the due date, they are as basic as credit cards come. If you don't have any special financial needs and only need a financial safety net to fall back on in case of an emergency, then this should be enough. Standard credit cards are easy to use and understand, which makes them an excellent choice for all kinds of users.

2. Reward Cards

As the name implies, this kind of credit card rewards you every time you use them. Commonly, you either get cashback, store discounts, or, in some cases, travel miles from different airlines. But unless you can verify that the benefits you gain from owning a Reward card surpass these often hefty costs, you should steer clear. Reward Cards are known to have relatively high-interest rates. If you are looking to settle a long-term debt, Reward Cards won't be the best option because you won't use the main feature. On the other hand, if you are a frequent traveler and much of your income is spent on purchasing airline tickets, it might be worth it to explore Reward Cards offered by your bank. But you should keep in mind that most banks will need you to have a robust credit score to be considered for this type of credit card.

3. Purchase Cards

Purchase cards are designed to make expensive purchases more affordable and accessible to everyone. Offering interest-free credit for a period, sometimes as long as 20 months, you can use this kind of card to furnish your new house without having to worry about the extra charges you would incur with a regular credit card. The key to reaping the full benefits of purchase cards is to commit to paying the monthly fees in full and on time. Otherwise, you risk losing the zero interest rate and will have to pay interest on your large purchases. If you want a credit card to use for cash withdrawals to pay off your standing debts, purchase cards are not for you because the interest rate on cash withdrawals can be quite high. As with Reward Cards, you need a good credit score to qualify for Purchase Credit Cards.

4. Credit Build Cards

Your credit score is a big deal, and it can limit your options when it comes to credit cards. If your credit score is in terrible shape, Credit Builder Cards can be of great help. A bad credit score can categorize you as a high-risk client. Banks use Credit Build Cards as a tool to help you get your credit score back on track by offering them at high-interest rates versus low credit limits. If you are able to commit to settling your Credit Build Card monthly bills in a timely manner, this will help creditors see that you are indeed reliable, and, little by little, your credit score will start to improve. Credit Build Cards can sometimes be a necessity rather than an option, for example, when you are in between jobs and don't have a steady income. Or if you're still a first-time cardholder who doesn't have the time to build a decent credit score. In such cases, banks and other lending institutions will lean towards the 'safer' option by offering you Credit Build Cards until you can prove that you are reliable enough for a higher credit line option. Unlike Reward and Purchase credit cards, Credit Build cards are only meant to build credit, and there are no extra benefits.

Tricks To Settle Your Credit Card Debts

Now that you have learned about the different types of credit cards and when to use each, here are some simple tricks you can implement to make sure you don't accumulate credit card debt.

- **Grow Your Income**

True, this is easier said than done; however, finding ways to grow your income is the easiest and simplest way to settle your credit card debt. You can pick up extra shifts or turn a side-hustle into a revenue-generating business. Not only will you become debt-free, but you will also be enhancing your financial situation and building healthy savings.

- **Reach For your Debit Card First**

While credit cards offer more convenience, debit cards are safer. Yes, they might not be a valid choice in many cases like online shopping, but, whenever possible, reach for your debit card before your credit card. By spending what you have, you limit any extra charges.

- **Seek Bank Advice For Alternative Solutions**

Like most banks, your bank probably provides a myriad of services that you know nothing about. If you are worried about your growing credit card debt, it might be time to pay your bank a visit to understand your options. Term loans, overdrafts, and balance transfer programs are only a few of the alternatives that you can use to settle your debts.

When used right, credit cards are excellent financial instruments that anyone can benefit from. However, the most important thing is to find the type of card that suits your needs and can help you settle your debts instead of adding to them. In the next chapter, you will learn more about the different kinds of debts and how you can deal with each to take you a step further in your financial security journey.

Chapter 6: Secured and Unsecured Debts

In order to wrap up this section of the book, we will learn the difference between secured and unsecured debts. As part of your getting out of debt initiative, you will need to be able to identify the kind of debts/loans you are dealing with to figure out the best way to approach them. This chapter will take you through the benefits and risks of both types of debt and how to manage them. Let's first start with the basic definitions:

Secured Vs. Unsecured Debts

Although there are many kinds of loans, they can all be categorized into either secured or unsecured.

With secured loans, banks and other lending institutions can only approve your loan request with collateral. This can be in the form of an asset that your lender can claim in case of your inability to repay your debts. As for unsecured loans, the lender offers you the requested amount without asking for collateral in return. This means that the lender is bearing the risk of you not ever being able to pay them back. Here, a lawsuit is sometimes necessary for the lender to collect the debt that you defaulted on. Given the associated risk, you won't be surprised to learn that an unsecured loan's interest rates are much higher than those of a secured one. Moreover, only those with an excellent credit score and solid credit history can enjoy the financial freedom that comes with unsecured loans.

In order to learn what's at stake with each type of loan, here are the most common examples and how can you use them efficiently:

Secured Loans

Secured loans which almost anyone can benefit from can be any of the below:

Mortgage: A mortgage is one of the most popular types of secured loans. Mortgages give you the opportunity to afford your own house that is within the constraints of your income. But, the bank or lending institution that provides you with the mortgage is technically the real owner of your home. Furthermore, when you combine the monthly interest that accumulates over the years, you will realize that you are paying a huge mark-up on your house's original price. If you can't do without a mortgage but want to mitigate its risks, you should:

1. Research different mortgage deals and try to find the lowest rates that you can comfortably pay off each month.

2. Secure a mortgage first and then go look for a suitable house to match. Don't do it the other way around or you risk wasting time looking at houses that you cannot afford.

3. Avoid making big purchases right before you are granted the mortgage. New debt on your credit balance can cause your mortgage provider to rethink your application and possibly decide against approving it.

4. Once you get the mortgage, make timely payments a priority. Not only will this help build your credit score, but it will also expedite any future loan requests that you might need.

Car Loan: With the considerable rise in car prices, many people can't afford to buy one in cash and need to apply for a car loan. Car loans are another type of secured loan where the ownership of the car acts as collateral to secure the lending party's rights. If you want to avoid risking the loss of your brand new car, you should make sure to keep the following in mind:

1. Like with a mortgage, you shouldn't spare any time or effort in researching the available cars in the market until you can find a loan that suits your financial situation.

2. Try to find a car loan that you can comfortably pay off as soon as possible. Dragging car loan payments out for years can more than double the final price for a car that is already deteriorating in value.

3. Pay attention to the fine print and any loan conditions that many lending institutions try to push on you. It's best to have an experienced lawyer review the loan contract and other related documents to avoid falling victim to a lousy deal.

Unsecured Loans

Credit Cards: Credit cards that we use every day are a great example of a collateral-free loan. When banks or any other financial institution issues you a credit card, they are basically giving you access to money that they can't guarantee ever getting back. However, with the credit limit in place, the lender can at least protect their money. You have already learned about how to best use credit cards in the previous chapter. However, here's a quick recap:

1. Shop for the right credit card to avoid wasting money on features that you won't use.

2. Always make sure you are earning more than you are spending to remain in a cash surplus position rather than a deficit.

3. Settle your credit card as soon as possible and don't wait until the due date. Doing this will help to keep your credit score intact.

Unsecured Bonds: Also known as debentures, unsecured bonds are financial tools issued by the government or big companies. Since these bond-issuing entities are more than financially capable, they can afford to offer such high-risk funds to the public. Helpful tips for using bonds more efficiently include:

1. Opt for short-term bonds over long-term ones to collect a decent yield with average risk.

2. Consider the buy-back policy of the bond-issuer to compare between different types of bonds. The buy-back policy gives bond issuers the right to call back their bonds if they perform poorly in the market and quickly lose their value.

3. Make sure you are dealing with trustworthy bond-issuers. It helps to look at their performance history and forecasted performance report before you can make any decision.

Now that you learned about the difference between the two types of debts, it's time to move forward to the next chapter where you will use this information to better understand how to borrow money more efficiently.

Part Three – Create Financial Security

Chapter 7: The Best Way to Borrow Money

Everyone aspires to have financial stability in their lives to at least afford the necessities and maybe treat themselves every once in a while. However, some people can suffer from periods of financial instability that lead them to struggle to make ends meet. This can be for a variety of reasons, but it eventually leads to them not being able to afford the necessities until they can get their life back on track. During such times, people may need to resort to borrowing money. Here are a few of the ways you can borrow cash to get financial security until you can get your cash flow back on track.

Credit Cards

Getting a credit card is one of the easiest and most common ways of borrowing money. If you are facing a cash emergency, credit cards offer quick and easy access to cash and can help improve your financial situation if you repay your credit without any delays. There are two types of credit cards out there that individuals can benefit from, depending on their situation.

Zero Percent

Many people shy away from credit cards because they fear they will end up putting themselves into more debt instead of solving their temporary financial issues. But one can get out of the financial turmoil as well as not have to deal with interest-laden debt by choosing a zero percent credit card. Those are made for people who want to use small amounts of credit just to get out of their temporary money troubles and who can prove they had a solid financial history before their issues started. If they meet the eligibility criteria, they can borrow money without having to pay any amount of interest as long as repayments are promptly made.

Regular Credit Advance

For those who have steady jobs and a regular income but are facing unprecedented money issues that can be resolved with just a bit of extra cash, a regular credit card advance can be the best way to go. You will get the money you need, provided you pay it back in installments agreed upon with the lender. You will also have to pay an interest rate that depends on how much money you are borrowing, as well as the interest rates of the lender themselves. Your credit history may also affect the interest rate you receive on your loan.

Personal Loans

If your financial situation is too great that a simple credit card advance cannot solve it, then you may need to opt for a personal loan. These loans vary in their amounts, but they tend to start high and go higher. You can apply for a loan and pay its amount back to the lender over the duration of many years, depending on your agreement with the lender. These are the two most popular options for unsecured personal loans where you will not always need collateral to obtain the money you want to borrow.

Credit Union

Members of certain groups or organizations tend to

have their own credit unions that aim to help those who are members if and when they find themselves in financial turmoil. These are usually non-profit unions that work in the same manner as banks when it comes to lending any of the members a sum of money. They may not have the same amount of features and services provided by certain banks, but they can certainly come in handy to their members who may be looking for fair rates when borrowing cash.

Bank

Another common way of getting a personal loan, which many people prefer, is through banks. They offer a variety of loan options that do not have to be secured by collateral. It is a traditional and safe way of borrowing money without having to worry about how secure it will be in the long run. However, you will not get as much leeway paying back your loan once you start getting your finances back on track. You will need to pay everything back on time, or you may end up having to pay huge interest rates and harming your overall credit score.

Home Equity

Those wanting to get big loans for any purpose, be it because they are in financial trouble or looking for big investment opportunities, may find it best to choose home equity options. These options are made for people who own homes and borrow money that they can repay over a long time. Interest rates are relatively low with this option, and people can browse through banks to see who can offer them the best loan options if they re-mortgage their homes. It is a great way of cashing out money quickly and smoothly without having to worry about making big payments back too soon. But be careful as you are putting up your home as collateral.

Peer to Peer Lending

For some people, borrowing money from official organizations and banking entities does not sound like the best idea. Instead, they would rather depend on their social circle to get by and borrow any cash they need to get through their financial problems. Peer to peer lending options may be the best idea for those people as they will not have to go through official organizations or middlemen. There are now online platforms that connect lenders to borrowers through secure lines where they can do their transactions away from any financial institutions.

There is no one right way to borrow money. Everyone's needs and preferences are different, and with that, their choices in loans can be different too. In order to decide on the best borrowing option, you need to assess your situation and decide on the amount of money you need before doing extensive research. There will always be different deals with different lenders, and it is essential that you do enough research to find those deals.

Chapter 8: Making Wise Investments

Once you settle your debts and have a cleaner financial slate to work with, it's time you start thinking about building your financial security. Finding the best ways to invest your money is an essential aspect of that security if you want to live a comfortable life and have a bigger chance of a lucrative retirement. Many people make the mistake of rushing into investments that they don't understand. However, given the risk of losing one's entire life savings, investing is an extremely critical decision. This chapter will teach you how you can evaluate investment opportunities to decide which ones would be considered wise versus those you should avoid. In addition, you will be introduced to various investment options and the properties of each.

What Are Investment Opportunities?

There is a wide variety of investment options that you can choose from to grow your money. The best investment options are those that offer high profits and low risk. However, in today's turbulent global economy, this combination is a rarity.

Most people prefer stability over higher returns. Such is the case with the new digital currency market. Although it yields higher profits, many see the associated risk as a turnoff and prefer to stick with more traditional investment ventures. For years, people have gravitated towards stocks, real estate, and pension funds, which explains why these common avenues are still going strong. Let's explore each further:

Stocks

Arguably one of the best ways to make money is by trading in the stock exchange market. However, it does require a certain level of knowledge if you don't want to waste your money purchasing random stocks. You will also need to have reliable sources, whether in the form of an experienced financial advisor or a beginner-friendly software that can help you navigate the stock exchange world. Before you decide if buying stocks is the right investment option for you, you should consider the pros and cons.

Pros

1. High yields.

2. Easy to understand with some practice.

3. You don't need a huge lump sum to get started.

4. You can access your returns at any time.

Cons

1. Equally high risk.

2. The stock market is very unpredictable.

3. Takes time before you can have a decent return on investment.

For every stock investment opportunity that presents itself to you, make sure you weigh the pros against the cons before you can decide if it's a wise investment or not.

Real Estate

In most countries, the real estate market is

constantly growing, making it an attractive and highly reliable investment option. If you direct your attention towards new up-and-coming neighborhoods, it could be a good chance for you to make a lot of money. As with stocks, real estate investment is not for everyone:

Pros

1. Control over your property and assets no matter where they are.

2. You make a guaranteed monthly income as long as you have tenants.

3. Having an insured property means that you can receive tax benefits.

4. You can benefit from your property at any time. For example, if you are moving out and need somewhere to stay until your new place is ready, you can always use your rental property.

Cons

1. You will probably have to deal with the hassles of acting as a landlord.

2. During periods of vacancy, your property can be a liability.

3. Hard to liquidate. You can't count on your real estate property in case of a financial emergency when you are in need of fast cash.

Pension Funds

Investing in a pension fund is a smart way to guarantee a more comfortable retirement. Thanks to its long-term nature, you can live a lifestyle in your golden years that you would've never afforded any other way. As the younger generation is becoming more aware of the importance of retirement planning, there has been an increase in the variety of pension fund investments available in the market. Investing in pension funds can be a bit controversial; however, consider the following before you can decide where you stand.

Pros

1. It's a long-term plan which guarantees a proper annuity for a steady cash flow that you can benefit from as a retiree.

2. It gives you the option to choose your preferred payment method. You can choose to pay a big amount upfront or divide it on installment-basis.

3. You can make emergency withdrawals from your pension fund if you need cash for an unexpected crisis.

4. When you invest in pension funds, you diversify your investments across different assets which can help you minimize your risk considerably.

Cons

1. For pension funds to be worthwhile, you need to start investing from a young age. This could be a challenge for younger people, as many start accumulating savings later on in life.

2. The annuity you accumulate over the years is subject to tax.

3. Although pension funds are entitled to a tax deduction, there is a maximum limit to the amount that can be deducted.

Working with a financial advisor, you can come up with a good financial plan that uses a mix of the above investment options to guarantee the best results. However, you can still benefit from the following if you want an easy and straightforward way to identify a wise investment:

- Identify your goals. Think about what you are looking to gain from your investments and then find the assets that best match your needs.

- Study the market of the financial instrument you are considering. If you notice an upward trend over the years, this is usually a good sign.

- Have a reliable source of information. Don't believe anything you read in a random article or a 'tip' that your colleagues from work share with you. Instead, subscribe to one of the major financial publications and reach out to market experts for valid information that you can confidently use.

- Always remember to factor in taxes when evaluating an investment option. At the end of the day, you want to be able to compare the net profits you yield from each investment type.

- As much as you can, diversify. If you don't have the required financial expertise, try to eliminate the risk by spreading your money across different investment ventures.

Understanding how to evaluate the worthiness of your investment options will give you control over your financial life. It's essential to digest all the information you learned in this chapter to prepare you for the next one where we will discuss how you can best prepare for retirement.

Chapter 9: Preparing for Retirement

If we are to cover all aspects of financial security, we can't leave retirement out. If anything, you need to start planning and saving for your retirement as soon as possible. As soon as you build financial stability in your current life and clear out debt, it's time to address the crucial topic of preparing for retirement. Here's how you can plan for retirement effectively and efficiently.

Plan According to Your Age

It's never too late to start planning for retirement, but it's never too early either. In fact, the sooner you start, the better the financial security you can achieve. You'll never believe how significant the few bucks you save early in your 20s can become; never underestimate the power of compounding, especially in the long run. Depending on when you start planning, your approach will vary significantly.

To build your retirement strategy on a solid base, you'll take both your current and expected retirement age into consideration. The bigger the gap, the more time and options you'll have. For instance, starting in your later years with less than 10 years to save for retirement may limit you to safer kinds of investment, such as bonds and other securities. On the other hand, you won't have problems investing in fluctuating stocks if you still have more than 30 years ahead of you. Starting earlier in life means that you're investing for the long run, so short-term fluctuations won't be significant in your portfolio.

Keep in mind that inflation can destroy the value of your savings. Even a low inflation rate can keep accumulating over time and take away a huge portion of the value of your savings. That's why it's empirical to keep revisiting your plan across different phases of your life or after major economic fluctuations. That way, you can find a way for your returns to outweigh inflation.

Make Realistic Expectations for Retirement

Do you believe you'll spend more or less money after retirement? Many people make the mistake of estimating too little annual expenditure when it comes to retirement. Their argument will go like this: you won't need to spend money on transportation, work expenses, and other daily costs endured in the busy lifestyles they're living. Is that really realistic, though?

If you look at it from the other side of the argument, you'll realize that you'll have so much more time on your hands after retirement. You'll be free to explore your city, travel, buy luxury items, spend money to fill up your time, and catch up on everything you missed out on throughout your pursuit of your professional life.

You'll have to set very realistic expectations for retirement, which depends on your post-retirement spending habits, as that's the first point in calculating the size of your retirement portfolio. Instead of estimating an annual income of 70% to 80% of the current annual income, it's better to make it as close to 100% as possible. That's especially critical if you'll still be making payments for outstanding debts or other expenses during your retirement period, such as paying off an ongoing mortgage or paying for your children's tuition fees. Better yet, it's advised to create a bigger margin for unexpected situations.

Don't forget that you'll be older during retirement, and old age comes with its own needs and requirements. In the case of chronic medical conditions, treatment regimens, physician appointments and follow-ups, and prescription medications, you should factor more money into your calculations. Also, advancement in medicine has elongated humanity's average lifespan, so make sure you do your calculations correctly so you don't outlive your savings.

Divide Your Retirement Portfolio According to Needs

Your retirement plan will be broken down into multiple divisions according to your needs. For starters, you'll want to designate a part for investment, whichever form you decide upon. This part will mostly be secured the closer you get to retirement age, and you should never, under any circumstances, break the security to cash out from it. The longer you keep it untouched, the more profit you'll get during your retirement.

Next, you'll want to designate a portion of your savings for outstanding payments. This part will include the mortgage payment, children's tuition fees, and other expenses that you'll need to cash out on periodically. This portion should be available in its liquidity, so you can make regular withdrawals without suffering any penalty.

Finally, you'll have a division that you keep making regular contributions to. This is where you save your extra bucks to compound their benefits over time. In conclusion, your plan should cover your needs across different phases and time horizons, providing the needed security, liquidity, and contribution option at any given time. Needless to say, you'll need to keep rebalancing your portfolio as you move from one time horizon to another.

Calculate After-Tax Rate of Returns

Don't make the mistake of counting your savings without subtracting the taxes. After all, the real feasibility of your portfolio can only be assessed after calculating the after-tax rate of your investment returns. You may think that it's enough to settle for a 10% return rate if you're investing for the long run, but you'll soon realize how unrealistic that is if you cut out the taxes. These taxes will vary according to the type of retirement account you've opened, so make sure you're aware of your tax status before you withdraw funds.

Estate Planning

Your retirement portfolio will never be complete without a solid estate plan in place. Your estate plan will protect the right of your beneficiaries to your assets after you've left them. The estate planning process is complicated and has different strategies depending on your current age, so it's best to hire an estate attorney to guide you through.

For people that work for a company, the business will take care of some of your retirement investments. However, just because your employer has opened a 401k plan for you, that doesn't mean you shouldn't go over it and check if it's going to fulfill your needs later in life. As for the rest of the self-employed people, they'll need to take care of the whole process on their own. Seeking the help of an experienced financial planner or an attorney can help them achieve financial security in their later days.

Conclusion

Efficient finance management doesn't require tons of experience or sophisticated knowledge. Having access to valuable information presented in a simple manner can help anyone gain control of their personal finances. And this is what you've hopefully learned from the effortless style and flow of ideas throughout this book's chapters. A blend of basic rules and more elaborate planning can be all you need to make change happen.

If you are struggling with your finances, you don't need to despair or accept living under stress all the time. It takes the willingness to take action and turn the situation around, but that is something that you are in full control of. The fact that you decided to pick up this book is indeed a step in the right direction. Whether you are still at the beginning of your career or you're already halfway towards retirement, it's never too late to start planning.

When you approach your finances in an organized and systematic way, it all starts to make sense.

In the first chapter, you were asked to set your goals. Everyone has different financial needs, so it was very important to define what you are to have a solid foundation to build upon. Then, in chapter two, you learned about budgeting principles and how you can use the current technology to simplify the budgeting process. By now, you should have a clear idea of how to create a smart budgeting plan to help you reach your pre-defined goals. Chapter 3 discussed savvy tips about how to be thrifty when it comes to the nonessential items and monetize your side hustle to earn extra money. The fourth chapter sheds light on your credit score, and then in chapter five, you were introduced to different types of credit cards and how and when to use each. Chapter 6 showed you the difference between secure and unsecured debts and how to use each to your benefit. Finally, in the last section of this book, you were given the tools to create financial security, from the principles of borrowing to learning how to differentiate between wise and unwise investments, to eventually preparing for your retirement.

As mentioned in the introduction, you will want to revisit these chapters time and time again whenever you're dealing with financial troubles and when things are going well. The ideas that you find in this book might be basic, but they're still extremely effective and tried and tested. Share the book with your friends and family to help them understand how you're planning on changing your life and how they can change theirs.

Money Management 101 makes an excellent Christmas gift for those around you who struggle to make ends meet. It's also a good way to stay accountable and have someone help you get back on track.

Don't put it off any longer. Make the decision to start now and marvel at how your life will change one step at a time.

References

https://www.investopedia.com/articles/personal-finance/100516/setting-financial-goals/

https://www.nerdwallet.com/article/finance/how-to-set-financial-goals

https://www.thebalance.com/how-to-make-a-budget-1289587

https://pulseapp.com/blog/5-ways-to-spend-less-and-make-more

https://www.moneyunder30.com/trick-yourself-into-saving-more-and-spend-less

https://www.instructables.com/21-Ways-to-Spend-Less-and-Save-More-Money/

https://www.experian.com/blogs/ask-experian/ways-to-spend-less-and-save-more/

https://www.moneyunder30.com/how-credit-works

https://www.upgrade.com/credit-health/insights/complete-guide-to-credit-scores/

https://www.creditcards.com/credit-card-news/history-of-credit-cards/

https://kclau.com/wealth-management/reduce-credit-card-debt/

https://www.moneytalksnews.com/8-golden-rules-mortgage-shopping/

https://www.cnbc.com/2014/09/15/car-loans-5-tips-to-get-the-best-deal.html

https://goldenpi.com/blog/essentials/bond-market/factors-to-consider-while-investing-in-bonds

https://www.foxbusiness.com/money/cheapest-way-to-borrow-money

https://www.uswitch.com/loans/guides/whats-the-cheapest-way-to-borrow-money/

https://www.businessinsider.com/personal-finance/how-to-borrow-money

https://www.greateralliance.org/the-best-ways-to-borrow-money-during-a-crisis/

https://economictimes.indiatimes.com/wealth/invest/top-10-investment-options/articleshow/64066079.cms

https://www.moneyunder30.com/how-to-invest

https://www.outlookindia.com/outlookmoney/investment/advantages-disadvantages-of-pension-plans-4357

https://www.fool.com/investing/2020/06/27/the-pros-and-cons-of-investing-in-stocks.aspx

https://economictimes.indiatimes.com/wealth/invest/pros-and-cons-of-investing-in-nps-for-retirement-saving/articleshow/75914169.cms?from=mdr

https://www.moneyadviceservice.org.uk/en/articles/top-tips-for-choosing-investments

https://www.dol.gov/agencies/ebsa/workers-and-families/preparing-for-retirement

https://www.merrilledge.com/article/7-steps-prepare-for-your-upcoming-retirement

www.ingramcontent.com/pod-product-compliance
Lightning Source LLC
Chambersburg PA
CBHW070458220526
45466CB00004B/1875